365 DAYS OF DEPRESSION

Days 1-50

Yousef Zaki

Day #1

Today I woke up.

I didn't sleep enough last night;
it was just 4 hours.

I woke up on a work call ... the
worst way to wake up.

There is always something I
forgot or something broken or
something that makes you
worry or anxious.

The worst thing in social or work
relationships is that you can't
tell your fears, sadness or
burdens ... you have to fake
power while defeated from
inside ... your mind searches
every second for words,
phrases and expressions to
keep the conversation going and
to make sure that you don't look
like a freak

Everyone is waiting for you to be
a reasonable responsible

person, to act by the book ... no sadness, no pain, no despair, no running away.

No chance for the child inside you to cry, to shout, to declare that he was defeated ... you are an adult; you can't give up.

After a while you get used to that ... you hide everything and learn to live as a fake man. Your reactions aren't real. Your words don't express you. You let the society remove your difference to be exactly a "normal human" ... meanwhile, all your thoughts, all your opinions, all your cries, all your feelings are buried ... you are buried, and there is a strange version of you ... a shiny and society-usable version.

Day #2

I just saw a movie about (wall flowers) ... it was exactly me.

I saw in him my shy suffering self that people count its every step. The one that things never work out for.

But more importantly, I saw myself in the hole where all circumstances get together, simply inform you that there is no hope. Everyone gets distant, physically and emotionally and you are in the dark hole alone. A violent void if we may say. Heavy chains tie you and a huge rock settles on your chest.

But nobody is around you. The others are far away ... you are in your own universe yet you aren't its god but you are a hopeless slave.

The thoughts ... thoughts stalk and surround you. They get a face-to-face match with you. A flood of sadness and despair immerses you and any talk about hope is just an imagination.

Those are the moments that make you realize that life is unbearable. Suicide obsessions never leaves you ... they attack violently and don't let you even look away ... it is a war, my friend ... a war no one but you knows about. A violent war takes you unprepared. And enemy soldiers sneak in silence and discretion.

But the worst thing about this war is that it happens inside your mind ... nobody knows ... nobody feels ... it is just you who have to fight ... you don't have the right to surrender. You even don't have the right to shout. And of course, you can't protest ... that's your painful destiny and only you have to bear it.

Can you express that? ... can you tell others about that war? ... no

Because you are an adult and adults don't complain, don't get sad, don't take vacation. You will always have to run even if wounds cover your feet ... even if you have no feet at all.

day #3

conversations are killers.

Why do we have to talk in the times we don't want to?

Can't we someday answer their questions with a sign that says "I don't have any energy to talk now"?

Let's admit it, any conversation needs a psychological energy .. no matter how the conversation was simple or with non-threatening person ... but it still needs some psychological power.

In many times, you find yourself inside the conversation, so you can't prepare for it in advance like you usually do ... you are in here and trapped.

Your words will be floppy, the phrases will be bumpy, some stuttering. You will repeat some expressions with no reason but they are the only ones you find on your tongue ... every second you wish to end it, as every moment presses your nerves and pumps tons of adrenaline in your blood.

Some people will notice your fear and hesitation. Some will ignore it and some will get advantage of it. But some won't even notice, and I wish everyone becomes like that.

Day #4

Phone calls ... a hell.

For years I thought that I'm the only one who shivers when the phone rings ... but I knew we are many.

I ignore phone calls frequently, for nothing but to maintain my psychological peace ... in another words, to avoid any possible stress or tension.

As far as I remember, no phone call got me any sort of happiness ... there is always a problem has to be solved, someone require a favor or an opinion, some people blame you for something you did or didn't do or some of them force you to go out with them.

Nothing good ever comes from phone calls.

How can you explain to them how terrified you are from their calls? How can you explain that it became something close to a phobia?

The situation becomes worse when you work in a profession where you can't turn off your phone ... I envy those people who can do that.

I'm obligated to keep my phone on 24/7/365 .. I don't have the privilege of choice.

And if I decided to rebel and turn it off or ignore calls, from nowhere I find disasters fall on my head, lightening hit my world and I drown in mud to my nose.

Day #5

Social media makes a siege around you, especially chatting apps.

Every notification is a heavy burden.

You are not free to be alone. There are a thousand person are waiting for a reply to their messages. A thousand person are stalking you. A thousand person disapprove your reactions.

So, instead of being a reason for comfort and entertainment, social media is becoming more and more overwhelming and exhausting. You have to complement, to be double-faced and to be available all times for anyone you know or not even know.

The least human right is that
you can choose your suitable
time to answer message or even
choosing not to answer at all.

It is your life. Who give others
the right to force you to do
things the way they see right?

Let's disable notifications ...
may we find any sort of peace.

Day #6

How to respond to people compliments and cliches?

How to cope with conversations' boring common phrases while we can't even talk?

Can people imagine how much energy I need just to release one word from my mouth?

I don't want to continue talking or even start ... but I have to. Otherwise, I will be accused of rudeness or may be even madness.

Fear of social rejection is more powerful than any attempt to be different or any objection to common communication forms.

But also to be fair, I would be offended too if someone refused to continue talking to me ... maybe that's why I used to

continue conversations when I
don't want to.

Day #7

The critical point of every day is waking up time.

If you can leave your bed and put your clothes on, your day becomes good and productive.

If your depression tied you, you will feel like there are mountains of steel prevent you from moving. You will continue sleeping and wake up late on violent voices of guilt and inferiority in your head. You will hate and blame yourself a thousand times. And you will add your failure of waking up of that day to your long credit of failure.

It is so weird what can a few minutes in the beginning of the day can do.

If you can get past them, you will be mighty. But if you can't,

your life will be much more black
and dead.

Day #8

Who the hell invented compliments?

Why *do you need to* fake happiness when others succeed while you are actually jealous or even don't care at all?

Why can't you be genuine and tell him it is a fake success or ignore their indirect request of emotional clapping so you can talk about what really matters to you?

Human relationships are really exhausting, and forced compliments are more exhausting and frustrating.

But I also don't tolerate rudeness or indifference from others ... I know it is an ironic contradiction ... but I am human ... I do exactly what I criticize others about.

Day #9

Loneliness is a good thing.

Being in a human-free well-ventilated place is a special sort of psychological comfort.

Being around people itself is a burden ... it takes a lot of energy and power ... even without having any conversations.

In loneliness, you are the emperor of time and place ... you do what you want with no pressure - mostly.

Just leave me and I'll be more than ok.

Day #10

Problems ... problems ... problems

From nowhere hills of problems come out; consecutively ... with no chance to catch breath.

Every time you think you managed to solve one, its siblings come from the unknown to laugh at your naiveness and helplessness.

Will the day come when we rest and wake up to a day with no problems? ... who knows?

Day #11

When responsibilities and deadlines accumulate, remember that you just need to be on survival mode.

Spare every effort just to stay alive ... forget for a moment all your career dreams, your weight, body shape or your money debts. Now, it is enough to be alive.

People won't realize what you are going through. They will wonder about your sudden silence. They will judge you and demand your ordinary reactions.

Ignore them my friend as they wouldn't understand. May be if they understand they would give you some slack. But who has the energy to explain?

The problem of worst events is
that they come during the
worst events.

Day #12

What if Hinduism was right?

Your life now isn't everything.

It is just a temporary period, you manage to live it anyway to come back as a bird or may be a butterfly.

Your life now is not the ending. There is a hope of a better, more comfortable and more joyful life … if you are still capable of tasting joy.

May be the universe isn't that unjust. Maybe life can be nicer.

It is just some more years. All what you have is to keep breathing … some air in, some air out and we are done.

Day #13

Life is so hard.

Why death is so distant?

If I died today, I won't regret anything.

Day #14

Nobody feels it.

There is a volcano of fear, terror, despair and sadness inside me. But I can't express it. I can't find words to describe my pain.

No one would care or pay attention. And if they do so, how would they respond to the tragedy that you are very weak, that you go into a Sisyphean struggle just to draw a smile on your face?

And what will they think of you? Will they accept you as you are? Will they pet your shoulder? Or will they increase your pain with criticism and advices?

Day #15

But no one can handle the fire of your internal dragon.

If they just let you unlock the gate, so the lava of your agony are released. No one would stand in the face of the screams.

They will run way from the horror that was hidden for years and years. They won't tolerate it. They wouldn't imagine that a human mind can hold all this pain, sadness, anger or despair.

No one would imagine ... no one.

Day #16

But my friend, sadness is eating
me from the inside.

It eats me that I have no cells
left to feel anything.

I became a flat human. No
depths, no feelings.

Just a stagnant pond of
nothing and on its surface
floating some sadness, some
pain and some of self-contempt.

Day #17

Life is terrifying, my friend ...
very terrifying.

A lot of changes, a lot of events,
a lot of decisions need to be
made, a lot of potential
disasters.

Every morning I wake up and ask
myself: what are today's
disasters and can we avoid
them?

Day #18

You have to be a warrior. There is no other choice in life.

Refusing to enter the battles is a choice you don't have.

It is just a fantasy I wish it was possible.

Everyone will say you worry more than you should or you over stress yourself. But they don't experience that feeling of anxiety and fear that eats you alive.

When you are eaten alive, you become like a human camouflage, shreds of flesh ... a zombie ... a corpse that looks alive but in fact it is crippled and dead.

No other choice.

You can't run away from battles and you can't afford to lose

them. Life doesn't spare any
place for losers.

If you become a loser then you
deserve nothing.

You have to fight and to win ...
you are not free.

Day #19

Sometimes, all what you wish is to pull the plug.

Just one step and all the fear will stop, anxiety will end and sadness will disappear. I think I deserve that.

I deserve to get away from pain and worry that squeeze me every second.

I didn't choose them and I didn't get involved in them willingly, so why my destiny is to be tied to them forever?

I just want to run away, to escape from captivity and be free from torture.

Day #20

When you are depressed you see
life as it is.

No frills, no unpractical dreams,
no empty hopes, no pain killers,
no fake reality.

A life filled with despair and pain.

No comfort, no happy surprises,
no real pleasures.

just consecutive floods of
frustration, anxiety and
sadness.

Day #21

The worst thing in life is to realize that you are a burden to others.

And worse than the worst is that you marry to feel that your partner is a burden to you.

And the worst of the worst is to have children to deal with them -consciously or unconsciously - as a burden to you.

This child will grow to find the whole world fighting him. He will feel absolutely worthless. He will struggle every hour to be accepted. He will beg for people respect and admiration every minute.

And eventually, he will be still convinced he is just a burden. His value is nothing. No one

cares about him as a person, no
one wants him.

He will have no doubt that he is
a rejected and hateful being, and
nothing would ever can change
this image.

Day #22

No time for sadness … No room to digest the pain.

You have to swallow them, to bury your inner volcanos with the dust of faking.

You have to press "mute" to shut up your screams and put a neutral smile on the face.

The world won't pet you or accept your despair.

You have to run, to work and to be productive, otherwise you will be ripped in the chopper of life.

Day #23

Despite your ability to describe
what is going inside you,
sometimes you stand confused
in silence.

Words can't describe. Or maybe
your mouth muscles are
paralyzed and your hand fingers
are too weak to write a single
word.

There are degrees of black inside
you that don't know their way
out.

You stay in silence ... in
loneliness.

Day #24

You are alone ... completely alone.

Everyone will ask how you are.

Everyone will offer to give a hand.

Of all those, only a few really care.

And of those few, there are few who won't judge or criticize you.

And of all those, no one will understand or really feel you.

Not because they are bad people or don't love you, but because nobody can see what is actually going inside your soul.

Despite all your attempts to explain, despite all your efforts of framing your pain in understandable words, despite how many times you try to expose your sadness ... they

barely understand your
sufferings.

No one would see your internal
storms except who have his own
storm.

Day #25

They always say to me: love yourself.

How can I love this miserable self?

I think I hate it ... I hate its continuous weakness and pain.

I hate its constant need of struggling and fighting.

I hate the emotional stress I'm drowned in to my nose ... I can't breathe. I can't rest ... isn't there any end for suffering?

Day #26

There is some level of emotional pain makes you hurt that you forget your constant thinking of suicide.

You are in the vortex and you have no psychological space to wonder about the feasibility of your life.

What I realize now that thinking of ending life is a sort of dreams, and pain demolishes dreams.

It is a miserable conclusion, but it seems right.

Day #27

Why life has to be that hard?

Every day I wake up filled with
fear and sadness.

Not one day I wake happy or at
least rested.

Always fear ... always anxiety ...
always inability to leave bed and
face the terrors of the world.

Day #28

Every time I get pressed by life, I ask myself a quite reasonable question: why I continue to live?

I always tend to radically solve problems, so the question makes a lot of sense.

Not living is a great choice, and maybe it is the solution to all the fatigue and pain.

You can say I'm afraid or have a little will power, but that because you didn't experience what I've been through.

Imagine the hardest situation you lived, that situation is like a spoon to the sea I am in every day.

Day #29

Pain tears me apart and I have nothing to do to stop it. No one around me to complain to about what life is doing to me.

I'm not just suffering, I'm suffering alone. Life becomes an endless series of misery.

Imagine going to sleep and you know you are going to wake up in the same anxiety, fear and pain.

They would say, everyone suffers ... yes, they are right ... but not like my suffering.

No one experience deep sadness, screaming pain and hopelessness and stay alive ... not breathing but feeling alive.

If those rough feelings aren't temporary, then they are lethal.

If those were your everyday
feelings, then you are literally in
hell.

Day #30

May be the worst thing about depression is not just the bad feelings but also the restlessness that comes when these feelings go.

In the truce times between depression waves, you can't catch your psychological breaths .. you are afraid that hell would come back any moment.

You feel inside that you are unworthy of rest thus unworthy of happiness.

You think life will smile at you when your depression episode ends, but that turns to be an illusion.

Depression is like a predator animal. It continues to attack even in its weakness.

That is not fair but it is true.

Day #31

When the usual depression wave starts to fade, there is another sort of depression behind the curtains.

An inner absurd voice makes you feel guilty and keeps knocks in your head saying "you have become better. Now, you need to finish all missions you postponed during the last period. You have no excuses this time"

So, Instead of trying to enjoy the recovery period and gather your torn shreds before the next attack, you find yourself obligated to drag your wounded legs to do what you missed.

And while doing so, you find yourself in the middle of the new wave before you know it.

A terrible infernal cycle...

Day #32

I am afraid … I don't know why.

I was ok, an hour ago. Now I don't know what happened.

Anxiety does that to me from time to time. It seems like it comes with depression in one package.

From nowhere, my feeling of security evaporates. I feel lonely while violent winds hit my mind windows.

I am suddenly filled with fear … no explanation was provided.

An hour ago, I was satisfied with what I was. I didn't do anything … I didn't do anything.

Day #33

I am alone ... completely alone.

When everything calms, I am still here alone.

No one to complain my loneliness to.

Sadness overwhelms me and makes me life-blind. I can't escape sadness and no one to drain my pain to.

Returning home at night is scary. Not because of ghosts or demons, but because the empty cold silent apartment where there is no warm hug, no shoulder pet nor even a sound of human breath. Only the painful void exists. The void that penetrates inside me. The void I desperately try to ignore or distract myself with anything to avoid thinking of.

Day #34

Do you know what is the worst thing about restaurants offers? It is family offers or the offers for two or more.

The offers look good, but you have no one to share with.

It seems a silly thing, but it really isn't.

You look at yourself and wonder why all these people have ones to share with, but you don't?

You eat alone.

Day #35

No one would understand waking up suffering of depression patient.

It takes an enormous will power to get out of bed and escape its steely bonds.

No one would understand that there is a difference between laziness and depression paralysis.

Depression in the morning is like a violent WWE champion. It holds you down and tie your four extremities. How can you ever move?

Day #36

The problem of morning waking up is that all day scenario runs in your head ... a scenario consists of a thousand steps ... every step requires too much effort and energy and you don't have a shred of any.

You have to wake up to do all of these exhausting series of . steps.

You need enormous amount of energy to move from laying on bed-state to enter the day events cycle. Energy equals that of an atomic bomb.

And the evening seems to be too far... A million years far.

Day 37

Depression pain is different from ordinary pain, physically and psychologically.

The ordinary pain is like a stab from a sharp knife. Sever and intense but temporary and limited.

Depression pain is a confident experienced pain. it penetrates your psychological skin layers slowly. Layer by layer is cut and your blood is spelled one drop at a time. Depression knife reaches every existing nerve and not one could escape its dominion. A patient pain that doesn't get bored or tired and with endless working hours.

The blade penetrates you every day and every hour. Your screams aren't loud, but continuous.

Day #38

no one talks about how much depression patient suffers with the money.

You need money, badly. And yet you can't work.

No one will support you. No one will provide you with food and medicine for free ... nothing is for free in this life.

Even in the worst moments of pain, you have to get up and struggle every minute. You have to deal with unbearable situations because you have no other choice.

Day #39

There is a quick decision I need to make right now. As if I don't have enough anxiety to add the stress of a quick decision to.

Making decisions is one of worst things for depression patient because you will need to deal with the results of your decision afterwards. And who knows how would you be at that time and how would these results affect you.

Making decision -any decision- is a risky gambling. You are risking the possibility of a new thing to happen. How will you deal with that while you can barely tolerate your old stuff?

Day #40

Comfort is a far dream.

All I want is to put my head on
the pillow and close my eyes ...
I'm not greedy.

Fear is filling me of the
possibility of a thousand
disaster.

How do people live a life that is
sabotaged with constant
anxiety?

People, you are lucky.

Day #41

There is some kind of money I've to pay today.

I'm wondering if during the next hours I'll gather enough money to pay or I'll miss the due date ?

If I could get the money in the coming few hours, I will feel better about myself, I will eat good today, I will be able to go out with friends tomorrow.

Will I succeed? ... I have to, because failure feeling will destroy me.

Day #42

Maybe the worst thing about depression is loneliness.

Not just being away from others physically, but also emotionally.

You are in a completely isolated area, emotionally.

No one understands or feels you. Not because they don't want to, but what is inside you is indescribable.

Even if you are able to describe, all the words in the world will remain impotent and crippled.

Day #43

Is it too much to ask for a hand
to hold ours?

A mouth tells us that
everything will be alright?

Eyes look sorry for us and in the
same time confident of our
ability to overcome the
hardest?

A hug from someone who
doesn't ask for a thing nor
willing for a personal benefit? ...
a pure love hug?

Day #44

A dagger penetrates my chest.
A burning pain takes me.

I have to do thousand things,
meanwhile I can't leave my seat.

I just want to sleep to become
separated from life.

Reality is terrifying with no hope
to be better.

I wish I have wings so I can fly far
away.

Day #45

Depression paralyzes you.

it prevents you from moving, literally not metaphorically.

Even the simplest things like turning your head or moving your hand seem very hard.

Even when you feel muscle pain, changing your body position becomes an overwhelming mission. Frankly, sometimes you can't even do that.

Day #46

Depression enlarges things.

Anything that is simple or easy turns out to be a huge mountain.

You can't see the actual size of anything. Because the size of a thing is related to the energy required to do it, which makes everything in life; for depressed people is a constant suffering and permanent agony.

In depression, there is no such thing called "easy thing".

Day #47

No one will understand how the fear of future accompanies enthusiasm inside depression patient.

Maybe the coolest thing in life is being enthusiastic to something. But depression kills this feeling with a sharp sword of fear… fear that you start and won't finish; like what you did dozens of times before.

And the truth is, I couldn't complete most of the things I started. I really don't know if it is the real truth or the truth depression persuaded me of.

Anyway, I became a failure in my own eyes, a person who doesn't complete anything. And if it happened and I completed something to the end, it takes an expensive emotional cost that makes me hate it and

decide not to start anything
new again.

Day #48

One of the biggest influences on my negative self-image is that I started a lot of things but didn't finish.

Because, after the initial rush, comes a short interval of getting used to it. Then I bump into a rough interval of exhaustion … I try to push myself and force it to continue. But after a while, I can't keep on, as the tension becomes stronger than my resistance power. So, I completely leave the thing in order to catch some of my breaths.

And that's how I remain in the loop of enthusiasm, starting, self-pushing and surrender.

Day #49

For countless times in my life, I forced myself to do things that I hate.

The expression of "self-forcing" in my head is a synonym for a dark black void.

And the tragedy is, I have to keep forcing myself to do everyday things. Because there is no other way.

If I didn't force myself, I won't wake up from bed, I won't eat or go to work.

Even if in my mind, it is like volcanos eruption or earthquakes or even asteroids collisions, at the end, I have to force me.

Day #50

Is there a linguistic expression of being pained in silence?

Depression patient has silent screams of pain. He may even smile, telling jokes or laugh.

A total separation between the inner terrible void and the silent or maybe fun mask.

Imagine a cancer patient who have a 24 hours pain, how much would you feel sorry and sad for him?

Depression patient also is in pain the whole 24 hours, only he can't open his mouth.

www.ingramcontent.com/pod-product-compliance
Lightning Source LLC
Chambersburg PA
CBHW050052260726
48658CB00005B/1913